CRITTERS

To Al
from one Wretched Mess
to another

CRITTERS

ALEXANDER LOWRY

AFTERWORD BY

DAVID BROCKMANN

TURNSTONE PRESS

Turnstone Press
P.O. Box 1500
Santa Cruz, CA 95061

ISBN 0-932658-00-8
Library of Congress Catalog
Card Number 78-64450

Printed in U.S.A.

To: John and Emma Lou Young —
dear friends and avid
critter watchers.

All of the photographs in this volume are of wild creatures in the western United States. They were photographed for the joy of it and with a sense of wonder at the inherent beauty and dignity of all living things.

A.L.

Mule Deer, Yosemite National Park, California, 1961

Elk, Prairie Creek State Park, California, 1971

Steller Sea Lions, Ano Nuevo Island, California, 1969

Marbled Godwit, Monterey Bay, California, 1974

Black-crowned Night Heron, Monterey Bay, California, 1975

Anna's Hummingbird, Santa Cruz, California, 1972

Great Blue Heron, San Joaquin Valley, California, 1971

Great Blue Herons, Moss Landing, California, 1976

American Bittern, San Joaquin Valley, California, 1971

Sea Otter, Monterey Bay, California, 1975

Gulls with crab, Monterey Bay, California, 1971

Marbled Godwits, Monterey Bay, California, 1974

Sea Otter, Pt. Lobos State Reserve, California, 1970

Black-tailed Deer, Big Basin State Park, California, 1967

Black Bear, Yosemite National Park, California, 1974

Shore Birds, Monterey Bay, California, 1974

Avocets, Palo Alto Baylands, California, 1970

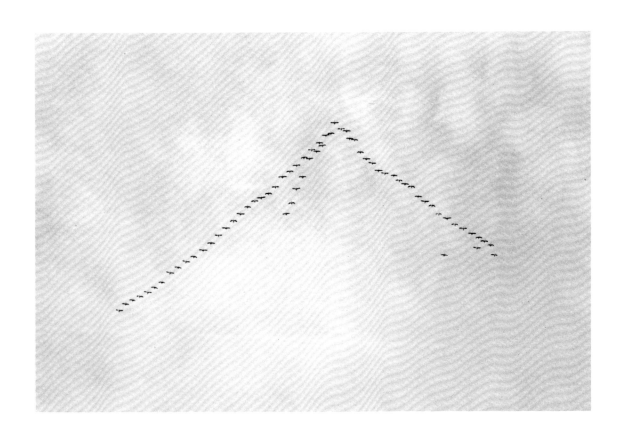

Snow Geese, San Joaquin Valley, California, 1964

3

Elk, Yellowstone National Park, Wyoming, 1974

Bull Moose, Yellowstone National Park, Wyoming, 1975

Steller Sea Lion, Ano Nuevo Island, California, 1967

Marbled Godwit, Monterey Bay, California, 1976

Sea Otter, Monterey Bay, California, 1975

Raccoon Family, Prairie Creek State Park, California, 1971

Barnacles, Santa Cruz, California, 1971

Ground Squirrel, Pt. Lobos State Reserve, California, 1971

Javelina, Aransas National Wildlife Refuge, Texas, 1976

Caribou, Mt. McKinley National Park, Alaska, 1965

Grizzly Bears, Mt. McKinley National Park, Alaska, 1965

Anemone, Pt. Lobos State Reserve, California, 1971

Dungeness Crab, Olympic National Park, Washington, 1976

Monarch Butterfly, Santa Cruz, California, 1977

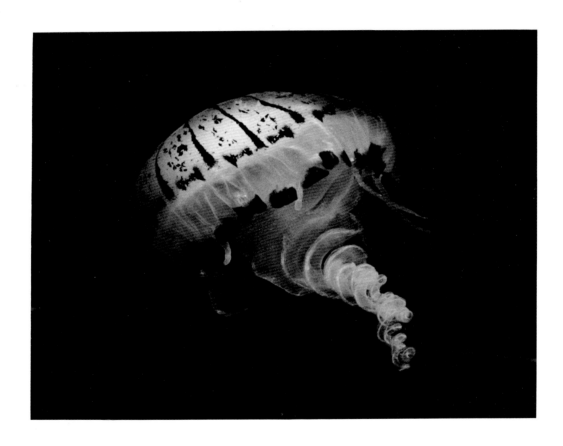

Jellyfish, Monterey Bay, California, 1974

Snail, Capitola, California, 1968

Black-tailed Deer, Big Basin State Park, California, 1967

4

Harbor Seal, Pt. Lobos State Reserve, California, 1971

California Sea Lion at door of abandoned light keeper's house, Ano Nuevo Island, California, 1969

American Bittern, San Joaquin Valley, California, 1971

Marbled Godwit, Monterey Bay, California, 1974

Dowitchers, Palo Alto Baylands, California, 1970

Willits, Monterey Bay, California, 1974

Western Gull, Pt. Lobos State Reserve, California, 1971

Brown Pelican, Monterey Bay, California, 1976

Dowitchers, San Joaquin Valley, California, 1975

Roadrunner, Big Bend National Park, Texas, 1976

Coyote, Organ Pipe Cactus National Monument, Arizona, 1976

California Sea Lion, Ano Nuevo Island, California, 1967

Gulls, 17 Mile Drive, California, 1969

Mourning Dove, Capitola, California, 1971

Brown Pelican, Monterey Bay, California, 1977

Bull Elephant Seal, Ano Nuevo Island, California, 1969

Whimbrel, Monterey Bay, California, 1974

Ernie Fenn

CRITTERS: ALEXANDER LOWRY

My association with Alexander Lowry began when we met as neighbors in Capitola, California nine years ago. Often as the sun came up over Monterey Bay he would be going off to photograph critters of the world as I was heading in the opposite direction to the world of newspapering.

My closest contact to his critter friends at that point came when our old cat Duane intruded on his bird photo sessions around his front yard bird feeder. It was then that I began to realize what was important to Al and how birds and animals motivated his lifestyle.

"I'm very much a Westerner," Al says, "although I've been exposed to some of the great cities of the world, I have always been more at home in the boonies. Many people are unable to relate to open space and the great outdoors like we do in the West. There are still wild places in the western

United States where one can encounter critters, particularly the large mammals, in their natural environment."

The unique thing about Al's critter photographs is that they are not mere likenesses but most often capture significant relationships within a species and between a species and its environment as well as individual personalities.

In 20 intensely busy years as a professional photographer, Al has worked for newspapers, magazines, book publishers, film producers, advertising agencies, universities and conservation organizations.

Born, raised and educated in San Jose, California, Al has photographed prize fighters and presidents, Paris in the spring and Hong Kong in the winter, and the Southwest in all seasons, but one of his great joys remains photographing the wildlife of the American west.

"I've been in newspapering a good portion of my life. As a kid I delivered papers, worked in the back shop, and even sold an 'extra' on the street corner on Christmas Eve. Working as a newspaper photographer is similar to working with wildlife. Many of the same skills are involved— being in the right place at the right time with the right equipment and being able to anticipate the action. I guess that photographing critters has been a balance for the things I had to deal with in newspaper work, although nature is no less violent.

"I am not at all interested in photographing animals in zoos; the only zoos I have seen are something between a circus side show and a prison and they depress me. I am as much interested in behavior as I am in physical appearance and no creature behaves naturally behind bars.

"Much of the challenge of photographing wild animals can come in getting to them—especially now, when their dwindling numbers make them harder and harder to find. It is almost always hard work, and sometimes dangerous." Often, it has required many hours of research, a great deal of physical effort and every photographic technique he has ever learned; and perhaps more important, it requires more patience than he ever thought he could muster. Once he stalked sea otters along the rugged California coast over a period of two years that resulted in only one picture to show for many hours and hundreds of exposures. With all the failures, however, the rewards of a single exciting negative or slide make his efforts all worthwhile.

"Through these pictures I'm trying to share experiences most people have never had. To me, it's very exciting and fascinating."

In addition to his varied career behind the lens, Al has led a number of photography workshops, produced books of nature photography, published articles and photographic essays and has exhibited regularly in museums and galleries.

Of all the animals he has photographed, birds excite him the most. "It's really funny about birds. Not too many years ago I was sure that bird watchers were really weird. Then one day I discovered I was one."

David Brockmann

PHOTOGRAPHIC NOTES

Of the 52 photographs presented here all but two were made with 35mm Pentax equipment. The exceptions were made with 2¼ by 2¼ twin lens reflex cameras.

More than half of the images were made with a 400mm lens which I consider my "normal" lens for wildlife work. A tripod, monopod or other support was used in nearly every instance.

Several brands of film are represented with Tri-X the most commonly used. It has become my standard film today, especially for long lens work. I normally rate it at 400 and develop in D-76 1:1. In low, flat light I rate Tri-X at 1200 and develop in Acufine.

Herald Printers
Monterey, California